On
Marriage
and
Family

H. JACKSON BROWN, JR.

Published in Nashville, Tennessee, by Rutledge Hill
Press, a Thomas Nelson Company, P.O. Box
141000, Nashville, Tennessee 37214.

Book design by Karen Phillips and Nikita Pristouris

ISBN: 1-55853-800-3

Printed in the United States of America

1 2 3 4 5 6 7 8 9 — 04 03 02 01 00

Introduction

A few years ago, I offered my eighteen-year-old son, Adam, this advice: "Choose your life's mate carefully. From this one decision will come 90 percent of all your happiness or misery." But after having chosen carefully, I added, the work has just begun.

A successful marriage, like a well-tended garden, takes constant care and loving attention. But the couple who spends the time to cultivate a joyful marriage and harmonious home discovers it is the best investment they can make.

Some of the entries in this little book include observations and suggestions I shared with Adam in both volumes of *Life's Little Instruction Book*. As a recent college graduate, he is giving serious thought to what it takes to be a good husband and father. He tells me these suggestions have been helpful. I hope you will find something of value here, too.

Men and women sometimes discover that finding a desirable marriage partner is difficult. That may be true. But there is another component to the situation: for it is not enough to *find* the right person, we must *be* the right person.

Choose your
life's mate carefully.
From this one
decision will come
90 percent of all your
happiness or misery.

*M*arry only for love.

*A*ll good marriages have
this in common: courtesy,
sacrifice, and forgiveness.

*D*iscover a special place to
watch sunsets together.

A successful marriage
requires falling in
love many times,
always with the
same person.

— MIGNON McLAUGHLIN

*A happy home
is a glimpse
of heaven.*

Kiss in the rain.

~~~

Slow dance.

~~~

If you've had a
hard day at the office,
save the complaining
until after dinner.

$\mathcal{N}$ever underestimate the power of forgiveness.

$\mathcal{P}$ut love notes under your spouse's pillow.

Grow old along
with me. The best
is yet to be.

— ROBERT BROWNING

$\mathcal{W}$hen you and your
spouse have a
disagreement, regardless
of who's wrong,
apologize. Say,
"I'm sorry I upset you.
Would you forgive me?"
These are healing,
magical words.

An archeologist is
the best husband any
woman could have.
The older she gets,
the more interested
he is in her.

— AGATHA CHRISTIE

$\mathcal{B}$e the first
to forgive.

~

$\mathcal{S}$end your loved ones
flowers. Think of a
reason later.

$\mathcal{L}$et your children overhear
you saying complimentary
things about them
to other adults.

$\mathcal{J}$udge your success by
the happiness of your wife
and the respect given to you
by your children.

*I*ntroduce yourself to your neighbors as soon as you move into a new neighborhood.

*R*emember that a good marriage is like a campfire. Both grow cold if left unattended.

$\mathcal{H}$old hands at the movies.

$\mathcal{G}$et involved at your
child's school.

$\mathcal{N}$ever leave a youngster
in the car without taking
the car keys.

$\mathcal{B}$uy your fiancée the
nicest diamond
engagement ring
you can afford.

Don't marry anyone
who won't bait their
own hook.

— WILEY DOBBS

...To have and to hold
from this day forward,
for better, for worse,
for richer, for poorer,
in sickness and in health,
to love and to cherish,
till death us do part.

— THE BOOK OF COMMON PRAYER

*R*espect your children's privacy. Knock before entering their rooms.

*A*lways buy electric blankets with dual controls.

*N*ever mention past loves.

$\mathcal{R}$emember the observation
of William James that
the deepest principle in
human nature is the
craving to be appreciated.

Marriage resembles
a pair of shears —
so joined that they
cannot be separated,
often moving in
opposite directions,
yet always punishing
anyone who comes
between them.

— SYDNEY SMITH

$\mathcal{P}$lant a garden together.

$\mathcal{N}$ever be the first
to break a
family tradition.

*How do
I love thee?
Let me count
the ways.*

— Elizabeth Barrett Browning

$\mathcal{A}$s soon as you get
married, start saving for
your children's education.

$\mathcal{P}$hone when you are
going to be late.

$\mathcal{L}$ive beneath your means.

$\mathcal{C}$onduct family fire drills.
Be sure everyone knows
what to do in case
the house catches fire.

$\mathcal{G}$ive children toys
that are powered
by their imagination,
not by batteries.

$\mathcal{D}$on't take good friends,
good health, or a good
marriage for granted.

*A*dd to your children's private library by giving them a hardback copy of one of the classics every birthday. Begin with their first birthday.

$\mathcal{D}$on't discuss
domestic problems
at work.

$\mathcal{D}$iscipline with
a gentle hand.

Love does not consist
in gazing at each other,
but in looking outward
together in the
same direction.

— Antoine de Saints-Exupéry

THREE THINGS TO LOOK FOR IN A SPOUSE:

1. a sweet disposition,
2. a sense of humor,
3. loves trips to Home Depot.

Let there be
spaces in your
togetherness.

— KAHLIL GIBRAN

$\mathcal{N}$ever yell at each other
unless the house is on fire.

$\mathcal{R}$ead the Sunday
comics together.

*L*ive so that when your
children think of fairness,
caring, and integrity,
they think of you.

~

*A*t least once a day tell
your wife how terrific she is
and that you love her.

*I*n disagreements,
fight fairly.
No name calling.

*P*ut love notes in your
child's lunch box.

*L*earn to say "I love you"
in sign language.

By all means marry.
If you get a good wife,
you'll become happy;
if you get a bad one,
you'll become a philosopher.

— SOCRATES

$\mathcal{R}$emember that
your child's character is
like good soup.
Both are homemade.

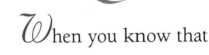

$\mathcal{W}$hen you know that
someone has gone to a lot of
trouble to get dressed up,
tell them they look terrific!

$\mathcal{P}$raise in public.
Criticize in private.

$\mathcal{R}$emember the two essentials
for a happy marriage:
separate bathrooms and
separate checking accounts.

A marriage makes of two
fractional lines a whole;
it gives to two purposeless
lives a work, and doubles the
strength of each to perform it;
it gives to two questioning
natures a reason for living,
and something to live for.

— MARK TWAIN

When you are away
from home and hear
church bells,
think of someone
who loves you.

Tell your kids often
how terrific they are and
that you trust them.

*R*emember that
no time spent with
your children is
ever wasted.

Love comforteth like
sunshine after rain.

— WILLIAM SHAKESPEARE

*D*on't worry that you
can't give your kids the best
of everything. Give them
your very best.

*I*n disagreements with
loved ones, deal with the
current situations.
Don't bring up the past.

Create a little signal only your wife knows so that you can show her you love her across a crowded room.

When playing games with children, let them win.

Never waste
an opportunity
to tell someone
you love them.

*R*ead to your children.

~

*S*ing to your children.

~

*L*isten to your children.

~

*R*emember that a good
marriage is based on
commitment, not convenience.

$\mathcal{D}$on't spend lots of time with couples who constantly criticize each other.

～

$\mathcal{M}$arry a woman you love to talk to. As you get older, her conversational skills will be as important as any other.

A good marriage
divides grief and
multiplies joy.

*B*e alert for
opportunities to show
praise and appreciation.

The husband who
wants a happy marriage
should learn to keep
his mouth shut and
his checkbook open.

— GROUCHO MARX

$\mathcal{N}$ever say anything
uncomplimentary about
your spouse or children
in the presence of others.

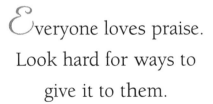

$\mathcal{E}$veryone loves praise.
Look hard for ways to
give it to them.

Cherish your children for
what they are, not for what
you'd like them to be.

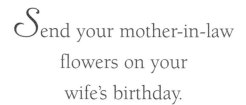

Send your mother-in-law
flowers on your
wife's birthday.

Remember that the best relationship is one where your love for each other is greater than your need for each other.

$\mathcal{D}$on't pick up after
your children.
That's their job.

$\mathcal{C}$arry a list of your spouse's
important sizes in your wallet.

$\mathcal{N}$ever forget the nine
most important words
of any marriage:

1. *I love you.*
2. *You are beautiful.*
3. *Please forgive me.*

*H*elp your children
set up their own savings
and checking accounts
by age sixteen.

*B*uy your spouse a year's
subscription to his or her
favorite magazine.

$\mathcal{T}$urn off the television
at dinner time.

$\mathcal{F}$lirt, but only with
each other.

A loving atmosphere
in your home is
so important.
Do all you can
to create a tranquil,
harmonious home.

$\mathcal{W}$hen you tell a child
to do something,
don't follow it with,
"Okay?" Ask instead,
"Do you understand?"

*A*pproach love
and cooking with
reckless abandon.

❧

*P*ut the cap back on
the toothpaste.

$\mathcal{T}$ake out the garbage
without being told.

～

$\mathcal{D}$on't expect others to
listen to your advice and
ignore your example.

$\mathcal{D}$on't let your family get
so busy that you don't
sit down to at least one
meal a day together.

Spoil your husband, but
don't spoil your children.

— LOUISE CURREY

*K*eep the porch
light on until
all the family
is in for the night.

$\mathcal{E}$ven if you're financially well-to-do, have your children earn and pay part of their college tuition.

⟿

$\mathcal{D}$on't expect your love alone to make a neat person out of a messy one.

Hold your child's hand
every chance you get.
The time will come
all too soon when
he or she won't let you.

*C*hampion your wife.
Be her best friend
and biggest fan.

*S*et aside your dreams
for your children and
help them attain
their own dreams.

Save an evening
a week for just you
and your spouse.

Believe in love
at first sight.

The love that we have in
our youth is superficial
compared to the love
that an old man has
for his wife.

— WILL DURANT

$Never$ walk out
on a quarrel.

$\mathcal{D}$on't judge people by
their relatives.

~~~

$\mathcal{N}$ever discuss
important matters with
the television on.

Love deeply
and passionately.
You might get hurt,
but it's the only way to
live life completely.

A successful marriage
is an edifice that must be
rebuilt every day.

— ANDRE MAUROU

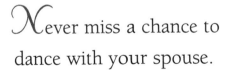

$\mathcal{N}$ever miss a chance to
dance with your spouse.

Surprise your wife
by vacuuming and
washing her car.

⌇

Never say, "My child
would never do that."

*W*hen a woman decides
she wants something,
don't underestimate
her ability to get it.

*K*now when to keep silent.

*K*now when to speak up.

*Marriage is
an empty box.
It remains empty
unless you put in
more than
you take out.*

I married my husband
for better or worse,
but not for lunch.

— LEIGH CARLETON

$\mathcal{G}$o on blind dates.
Remember, that's how I
met your mother.

$\mathcal{T}$ake good care of
those you love.

$\mathcal{S}$urprise loved ones with
little unexpected gifts.

*B*e your children's best
teacher and coach.

~

*E*very day look for
some small way to
improve your marriage.

~

*B*e romantic.

*W*hen a child falls and
skins a knee or elbow,
always show concern;
then take the time to
"kiss it and make it better."

*N*ever give a loved one a
gift that suggests he or she
needs improvement.

*A*llow your children to
face the consequences
of their actions.

*T*ake family vacations
whether you can afford
them or not. The memories
will be priceless.

$\mathcal{W}$hen your children
are learning to play
musical instruments,
buy them good ones.

~~~

$\mathcal{L}$et your spouse overhear you
saying complimentary things
about him or her
to other people.

*A*ttend your children's
athletic contests,
plays, and recitals.

A hundred men may
make an encampment,
but it takes a woman
to make a home.

— CHINESE PROVERB

$\mathcal{B}$efore going to bed
on Christmas Eve,
join hands with your family
and sing "Silent Night."

$\mathcal{H}$ug your children
after you discipline them.

$\mathcal{M}$emorize your spouse's
favorite love poem.

*R*emember that a woman
never gets tired of
hearing these words:

"I love you,"

"I cherish you,"

*"I'm so lucky
to have found you."*

*T*each your children the value of money and the importance of saving.

*N*ever type a love letter. Use a fountain pen.

*D*on't scrimp in order to leave money to your children.

*R*eally celebrate
your anniversary.
Make it an all-day event.

~

*B*uy a new tie to wear
to your wedding rehearsal
dinner. Wear it only once.
Keep it forever.

*R*emember that great love
and great achievements
involve great risk.

*L*earn to say "I love you" in
French, Italian, and Swedish.

$\mathcal{N}$ever buy a house
without a fireplace.

~

$\mathcal{D}$on't let family members
drive on slick tires.

$\mathcal{E}$xercise together.

$\mathcal{D}$ream together.

$\mathcal{P}$ray together.

If you can find a truly
good wife, she is worth
more than precious gems!
When she speaks,
her words are wise,
and kindness is the rule
for everything she says.

— PROVERBS 31:10, 26
(LIVING BIBLE)

$\mathcal{T}$ape record your
parents' memories of how
they met and their first
years of marriage.

A good husband
should be deaf, and a
good wife should be blind.

— FRENCH PROVERB

*D*rive as you wish your kids would. Never speed or drive recklessly with children in the car.

*M*ake the rules for your children clear, fair, and consistent.

*R*emember that a
successful marriage
depends on two things:
1. *finding the right person*
2. *being the right person.*

*E*very year celebrate the
day you and your wife had
your first date.

*E*ncourage your children
to have a part-time job
after the age of sixteen.

*N*ever stop the wooing.

*W*hen tempted to criticize
your parents, spouse,
or children, bite your tongue.

I chose my wife, as she did her
wedding gown, for
qualities that would wear well.

— OLIVER GOLDSMITH

Let your children see you
do things for your wife that
lets them know how much
you love and treasure her.

*O*pen the car door for
your wife and always
help her with her coat.

~

*D*on't overfeed horses or
brothers-in-law.

*W*hen angry,
never begin
a sentence with,
"You always..."

*G*reet each other
at the door with
a kiss and a hug.

I would like to have
engraved inside
every wedding band,
'Be kind to one another.'
This is the golden rule
of marriage and the secret
of making love last
through the years.

— RUDOLPH RAY

Be your mate's best friend.